The Trees Have Names

A Last Lecture by
Dr. Charles Hendrix

as transcribed and prepared by
Matthew Everett Miller

Copyright © 2017 by Matthew Everett Miller

All rights reserved under International and Pan-American Copyright Conventions. Gas Girl © DC Comics. The Red Devil logo, character and related images are trademarks of Reckitt-Benckiser. Cover image by Stockimo, United Kingdom.

Second Edition. Published in the United States.

ISBN: 1978416229 | ISBN-13: 978-1978416222

Contents

Introduction 9

A Last Lecture 55

The Auburn Creed 126

Acknowledgements 129

About the Font 131

About the Author 133

References 135

Now the Lord God had formed out of the ground all the wild animals and all the birds in the sky. He brought them to the man to see what he would name them; and whatever the man called each living creature, that was its name. So the man gave names to all the livestock, the birds in the sky and all the wild animals.

—Genesis 2:19-20 (NIV)

Introduction

Matthew Everett Miller

The idea for this book came to me not while sitting in Dr. Hendrix's last lecture in the spring of 2016, but a full year and a half after the fact, during the Reproduction course that Auburn students take in the third year of the veterinary curriculum. Professor after professor made reference to Dr. Robert Carson (Auburn University, Class of 1973)—a theriogenologist, cattle producer, and member of the Auburn faculty since 1979, who won almost too many awards and recognitions to list—in tones that were both glowing and nostalgic (Jeffcoat-Trant, 2015). Nearly every lecture, it seemed, contained at least one slide with some rule-of-thumb he came up with, or some truism he used to say. "I wish you all could have met him," one professor told us. "He was a truly remarkable man."

Dr. Carson passed away in March of 2015, shortly after his retirement following 36 years as a professor. I was never lucky enough to meet him or be taught by him, but the stories that his students and colleagues (now my professors) tell betrays the immeasurable impact he had on the college and the veterinary profession at large.

That impact, along with the struggle of my professors to sufficiently explain the full scope of the mind that had been lost, reminded me of something else. At the risk of drawing undue comparisons, that last lecture that Dr. Charlie Hendrix gave upon his retirement (about a year after Dr. Carson's retirement) seemed full of the exact type of stories I was lacking in trying to understand the legacy of Dr. Carson—rich, serious, funny, and expansive—the *why* behind the *what*. I imagined a generation of vet students in the not-too-distant future, hearing stories of Dr. Hendrix, the professor that I and so many others came to love, and naïvely asking, "Who is that? Who are you talking about?"

As a member of one of the last classes to ever learn parasitology from Dr. Hendrix, I felt it was my duty to preserve some of that history for past generations of veterinarians who knew him. And for the future generations, it is my hope to explain, however incompletely, just who Charlie Hendrix is and was.

Places shape people as often as the other way around, so it may be prudent to begin this story about Dr. Hendrix with a story about the place that came to define him.

In 1892, the Agricultural and Mechanical College of Alabama (which would be renamed Alabama Polytechnic Institute just 7 years later, and again, in 1960, to Auburn University) started a curriculum in veterinary medicine, led by Dr. Charles Allen Cary at the Agricultural Experiment Station. Fifteen years later, in 1907, the program became a fully-fledged veterinary college—the first in the South (the University of Pennsylvania being the second-most southerly vet school at the time). The college initially had three departments: Physiology, Surgery, and Veterinary Medicine.

In its early years, various faculty members conducted research which led to breakthroughs in major diseases like Texas cattle tick fever, hog cholera, tuberculosis, fowl paralysis and leukemia. In 1943, Lucille Sandahl Dimmerling became the first female graduate of the college, 43 years before the first black graduate—Donita McElroy—in 1985.

The vet school moved to its modern location (on Wire Road, to the southwest of town) in 1960 following the construction of two buildings—a large animal clinic in McAdory Hall and the Sugg Animal Health Research Laboratory—at the urging first of Dean Redding S. Sugg, then at that of his successor, Dr. James E. Greene. Bit by bit, new additions brought the campus closer to that which we know today. A 1968 gift from oil heiress Eleanor Ritchey, in combination with donations made 13 years earlier by field-trial dog competitor Kenneth Scott, funded the construction of the Scott-Ritchey Research Center. A small animal clinic (later renamed Hoerlein Hall) was completed in 1970, as well as a basic sciences building (later renamed Greene Hall) the following year.

There was a rush[1] in the '70s and early '80s, during which universities founded their own veterinary schools at an unprecedented rate, especially in the South (the first class of veterinary students was admitted to LSU in 1973, to Florida and Tennessee in 1976, to Mississippi State in 1977, to Virginia-Maryland in 1980, and to NC State in 1981), but by that time Auburn boasted a robust program that was naming its fifth dean and had already graduated 3,000 veterinarians.

The buildings kept coming: an imaging center in '87, the Raptor Center in '98, a lameness arena in 2002, and the large animal teaching hospital (named for Dean Tom Vaughan, whose article in

---

[1] Some have asserted that this vet school boom, which saw the number of American veterinary colleges grow by 35%—from 20 to 27— in just ten years can be largely attributed to the writings of English veterinarian James Herriot, author of *All Creatures Great and Small*, which was published in 1972. (Lowe, 1995)

the Summer 2017 issue of *Auburn Veterinarian* provided much of the source material for this section) in 2004. The 5,000th veterinary student graduated from Auburn in 1998, and by the time the Veterinary Education Center was completed in 2012, followed by the Bailey Small Animal Teaching Hospital in 2014, that figure had climbed to nearly 7,000.

The goals of the institution, it goes without saying, have varied (and multiplied) over time. Although Auburn's vet school was founded with some of the same goals as its contemporaries— namely food security and the reduction of diseases that left farmers of the day in financial ruin—it managed to survive the gradual decline that followed[2] (University of Pennsylvania, 1984).

---

[2] The number of American veterinary colleges open today—30 as of this book's publication—is actually lower than it used to be; 41 vet schools closed their

In the years afterward, Auburn continued to train veterinarians that filled the roles as they arose, by serving in the military, researching infectious disease, leading the charge in One Health, solving emerging problems in food safety and security, and most recently, filling the demands of the burgeoning small animal industry, which last year amounted to $15 billion in veterinary care alone (Addady, 2016).

Through all these changes, what has remained relatively constant is the dedication of the faculty not only to the students and the educational process, but to Auburn itself; once hired onto the faculty here, people tend to stay. Dr. Carson taught here for 36 years. Dr. Hendrix retired after nearly 35. Although both were impressive tenures, neither was what you'd call an outlier.

---

doors from the mid-nineteenth to mid-twentieth centuries, leaving just 18 open by 1959. (Boyd, 2011)

Dr. Ray Dillon (Texas A&M, Class of 1973) will have worked in the Internal Medicine service for 45 years by the time he retires in March of 2018. In 110 years as an independent college, Auburn has had just 7 deans—an average of 15 years each. Other vet schools for which I could find data ranged from 5 to 12 years per dean.

But as anyone who loves Auburn will tell you, their love for this place derives not from statistics like these, but from something unquantifiable, something more ethereal. They might tell you that, sure, people stay at Auburn a long time, but more importantly, there's a *reason* they stay.

Dr. Hendrix's last lecture can be viewed as a valiant attempt to explain this reason, to define the particulars of this love for Auburn, to give outsiders a sense of what that love means, however difficult that meaning might be to put into words. The postmodern writer David Barthelme said that truth is a hard apple to catch and a hard apple to throw. It seems to me that Dr. Hendrix, like so many others, caught an Auburn-colored apple a long time ago, and has been trying hard to throw it ever since.

The straight facts, as they relate to Dr. Hendrix, are easy enough: Charles Mackey Hendrix was born in Greenville, South Carolina the day before Halloween, in 1949.

His grandparents came from humble beginnings. His mother, Catherine, wanted to be a doctor back in the late '30s, but her father couldn't afford to send her to medical school, so she became a hematologist instead. At the tail end of the Great Depression, Hendrix's father (his name was Divver—a family name) wanted to go to Clemson, but like that of his future wife, Divver's family couldn't afford tuition either (he declined his father's offer to send him to the much-cheaper Furman). With only a high school education, Divver Hendrix, after serving in the military from '41-'46[3], made a living by doing taxes for friends and neighbors on an old typewriter in the winter. In the fall he officiated football[4].

I met up with Dr. Hendrix around five on a sunny Monday afternoon in September. He had been surprisingly difficult to get ahold of, which he explained, irritatedly, was due to a surprise update that had been pushed by the IT department about a week before, locking him out

---

[3] "I had two aunts who prayed my father wouldn't go anywhere dangerous. He never went anywhere at all. He flew a desk at Donaldson Air Force Base."

[4] One thing Hendrix learned growing up, he told me, was that "You never argue with a referee." Anecdotal examples were unfortunately not provided.

of his email completely. He'd spent most of the morning on main campus trying to sort the issue out. "You don't change things around on retired people like that," he said, shaking his head and echoing complaints I'd heard from him before about Canvas, Auburn's online education system.

But then his face melted into something softer, happier, as he said, "Oh, and my grandson." He'd been busy potty training Charlie, his daughter's 26-month-old child. "If you think teaching vet students is hard," he said, "try potty training a boy."

Both the first and second year classes had exams the next day (and third years had one the day after that), so with some difficulty, we found a free table upstairs in the hall of the VEC and took our seats in the wooden straight-backed chairs.

In his last lecture, Dr. Hendrix explains why he wanted to become a teacher. I asked him about something earlier: what made him want to become a veterinarian? He said it all went back to when he was just five years old, when he met two of his role models: Ernest Stewart (Class of 1950) and Herbert Riddle (Class of 1944). Both men were Auburn graduates who grew up in upstate South Carolina.

The latter was the father of W. Thomas Riddle (University of Georgia, Class of 1978), one of the founders of the Rood & Riddle Equine Hospital in Lexington, Kentucky. As a vet, the senior Dr. Riddle worked with large animals at Cleveland Park Animal Hospital in Hendrix's hometown and drove a yellow '88 Oldsmobile Delta.

Another man, who went by the name of Jack Chandler (University of Georgia, Class of 1969), provided mentorship for Dr. Hendrix as well. "He used to work me to death," he said. "But he was the first person to ever call me Dr. Hendrix, back when I was a vet student."

At times, that title may have seemed premature; during his first semester at UGA, Hendrix was hovering at a 2.0 GPA. The dean called him into his office and told him he had to raise that to a 2.25 by the end of his first year, and 2.5 by the end of his second.

He did graduate, of course, and in fact managed to pull a 4.0 during his last semester. Once he was out, he served for two years in the Army Veterinary Corps working in Dependent Animal Care, then in Food Inspection.

His service ended in 1976, which happened to be the nation's bicentennial. In celebration (of the bicentennial, not Hendrix's return to civilian life), the Ford Administration created a Bicentennial Commission, which created something called the Bicentennial Wagon Train, in which wagons and horses from all corners of the country converged on Philadelphia—where the Declaration of Independence was signed—for the July 4th celebration.

Citizens were free to ride along with the wagons on their personal animals, usually for a day or two. "But they had to be healthy," said Hendrix. When the wagon train came through Fort Gordon, Georgia, Hendrix asked for their EIA certificates[5]. "They said, 'We don't have any.' And all over the country, they had forgotten their

---

[5] Equine Infectious Anemia (EIA) is a viral disease of horses that is usually transmitted by biting flies. The Coggins test—which looks for EIA infections and was invented by Dr. Leroy Coggins (Oklahoma State University, Class of 1957) in the early '70s—is a standard requirement for interstate transport of horses in the U.S. (Larson, 2014)

certificates." When two mules on the wagon train tested positive for EIA, Hendrix reached out the large animal clinicians who'd taught him back at the University of Georgia. "I told them I had listened."

Hendrix's career ambitions had already been orbiting around the idea of becoming a teacher for quite some time, so after the wagon train, Hendrix went to the University of Minnesota to get his master's degree (and ultimately, his PhD). It was there that he met his research mentor, John C. Schlotthauer, who he discusses at length in his last lecture.

"I'm going to let you in on a secret. John always told me, 'Charlie, you are *not* a research scientist.' It took me a long time to realize what he meant, but eventually, I figured it out. He meant that if someone puts a beaker on the table right here, it's gonna be shattered on the floor a minute after that. I was a research screw-up, and he wasn't afraid to tell me."

Dr. Hendrix came to Auburn in 1981, the year he received his PhD. He told me, and presumably the hiring committee, that he did not come to Auburn primarily to do research (although his CV, forwarded to me by his daughter, shows 68 journal articles under the 'Publications' section, along with dozens of textbook contributions). He came to teach[6].

"We had a student one time looking at a wound," he told me, "and all of a sudden she saw something."

---

[6] To great success; he has won the Norden Award for Distinguished Teaching twice, in '84 and '88, and has been named Teacher of the Year by the Student Government Association on two separate occasions, in '87 and again in 2000. (Auburn University, n.d.)

Dr. Hendrix and the other veterinarian who was present, of course, knew what she was seeing, but instead of telling her, they let her look on her own and figure out what was there.

"She realized it was a screwworm[7]. Her face lit up when she realized she had made that diagnosis." That moment, for Hendrix, encapsulates what he has always loved about teaching: "I got to see the change in her face."

By this point in the interview, Hendrix had removed his watch and was fiddling with it as we spoke. I only noticed here, as he stopped turning it over and over in his hand. He looked at me, smile suddenly faded to something more opaque,

---

[7] *Cochliomyia hominivorax* is the scientific name for the screwworm, a parasite that feeds primarily on the flesh of warm-blooded animals, and is somewhat notable in that the maggots will also eat healthy tissue in addition to necrotic tissue. (Hendrix, n.d.)

and said, "Remember to look at people's faces. See what they tell you."

The interview wound its way along, and once I'd run out of questions to ask, the conversation descended (or maybe ascended) into a string of rapid-fire anecdotes that were only tangentially interrelated.

"I always say there is no crying in vet school, but there is weeping. We had a girl bawling her eyes out in the hall one time, and Josh Mann from the Class of 2007, was walking by. He put his book bag down and offered her a Kleenex. I went back to my office and wrote his mother a card."

At the time, I didn't know how (or whether) to incorporate these stories into the book, but I kept taking notes just in case.

"Oh, and Kecia Howell!" he said, remembering suddenly. "Class of '84. She was at my first lecture ever, and she came to my last lecture. When she was a student here, she went to see Paul McCartney in Tampa with 17,000 other people. She had made a Sergeant Pepper blue satin jacket and was sitting in the front row. Sir Paul saw her and asked her to come on stage and sing a song with him. At the end of the song, she kissed him. She came back to school and told me, 'Dr. Hendrix, his skin is so smooth.'"

And on like this—remembering the name of some student and jumping into another story almost before the smile had faded from the previous one.

After about twenty minutes, I have to say I was impressed. Sitting with him and listening to him ramble at length felt at times (especially when his eyes would light up with novel excitement) like conversing with an extremely precocious child with a penchant for story-telling. In truth, here was a man a few weeks shy of his 67th birthday, recalling names of people he hadn't seen in 30 years. He told me he got the ability, this superb gift of memory, from his mother, and passed it on to his daughter Charlotte.

Something else I gradually realized is that, in addition to being highly emotional stories, in which sorrow and joy often collide[8], the stories that most haunted Hendrix (and thus those he was most likely to remember and to share) were those that also provided some perspective: a student is crying but a bit of human kindness sets her right again; despite a stressful exam schedule,

---

[8] Take for instance the story of Luis Arguelles (Class of 1993) from Texas. He interviewed first at Texas A&M, where Hendrix says no one spoke to him outside the interview itself. You can probably guess how his interview at Auburn reportedly shone in contrast.

a student travels to another state for the experience of a lifetime.

I couldn't help but notice that when his stories shifted to the present, his tone darkened somewhat, betraying a disappointment—either gradual or all at once—that lay somewhere between those bright, hopeful early days of his teaching career and the present state of affairs.

Southern Florida saw an outbreak of screwworm last year among the native deer population, the first time the parasite had been seen in the U.S. in about 30 years (Guarino, 2016). In the 1960s, scientists from the USDA, many of whom were veterinarians, partnered with farmers, as well as local and state governments to mount a national eradication campaign against the screwworm.

It was the same organism Hendrix had watched a student joyfully identify years before. Veterinary parasitologists know (and like to think that their students know) that New World screwworms are easily identified by two darkly-pigmented tracheal tubes on the posterior end (the "rear end") of the larvae.

In covering the Florida outbreak, the Journal of the American Medical Veterinary Association published an image of the *anterior* end of the worm (the "head"), which lacks the distinctive bands that aid with diagnosis (JAVMA, 2017).

Hendrix said, "I gave them a call to let them know of their mistake. And when the woman had taken down my comments, I asked her how many other people caught that mistake. She said, 'Just you.'"

This answer troubled Hendrix. "I just don't understand my profession anymore."

The incident stood in contrast to his experience at the Bicentennial Wagon Train 40 years earlier. In both cases, he remembered something important, but in the case of the screwworm, he was evidently the only one to do so.

His disappointment wasn't just institutional; it was personal, too. His fourth year at Georgia, he went to do his preceptorship with a veterinarian he'd met some years prior. During the eight week program, an opioid called Demerol started coming up short at the clinic. Hendrix said, "And because I was so happy all the time, they thought it was me! They thought I was the one stealing it." Later on, when Hendrix was at Minnesota, he received word that the veterinarian who had supervised his preceptorship had overdosed on Demerol and died. He told me: "That broke my heart."

After a pause, he repeated something he'd said before: "I watch people. I look at people's faces." His regret here seemed to be that he'd failed to look thoroughly enough in the face of his mentor. He failed to see the suffering, failed to see what the faces were telling him.

"My dad taught me that," he said. "He always told me I should be able to look at myself in the mirror when I was shaving. 'Can you really look yourself in the eye? Is what you've done honest and right?'"

By this point, the sun was hanging low in the sky, casting long shadows on the floor of the two of us, facing each other at the table. There was a brief silence as he chose his next words carefully.

"I think y'all worry too much." He nodded as he spoke, convinced slowly then surely that what he was saying was true. "I think y'all want to call the shots too much. I wish we could be y'all. I mean look at this place," he said, gesturing around. "Everything is so perfect and sterile. It's like a gigantic womb. It's warm. There's a blood supply. Everything is safe."

He gripped his watch with both hands and ran his fingers against the leather again. Outside, the occasional car would park in the loop, and a vet student or two would emerge with engorged backpacks and surgery bags, then filter into the building.

"Y'all don't seem to understand that life isn't like that," he said. "To prepare you for life, we've got to be tough on y'all. We cut too many corners. When I was in vet school, when we'd do a physical exam on a cow, they'd sew a button under the tongue. Do you know why?"

I did know why; older students had told us that Auburn also used to employ this trick in the final exam for the Physical Diagnosis course. The idea was to make sure students were being extremely thorough in their physical exams, so as not to miss something subtle like an oral abscess (or a button)[9].

"And it worked. To this day, I have never forgotten that."

I had always assumed that the button trick was discontinued due to concerns for animal welfare, or perhaps a push by animal rights activists. Hendrix dismissed the validity of such protests when I brought it up. "The animal, unlike us, gladly endures what little pain there is for him."

---

[9] Two of the long-time coordinators for the Physical Diagnosis course at Auburn categorically denied that this procedure was ever done here. I was unable to verify whether Georgia has used the button technique at their vet school.

After that, we moved on to other topics, but every so often he'd drift back to this idea: "Everything comes too easy to y'all. It comes too easy."

At this point I should stop and acknowledge something that may be obvious to readers familiar with the profession: there exists a sizeable gulf between the sky-high baseline stress level of most veterinary students and the significantly lower level of stress that many faculty members believe we *should* be feeling.

It may seem quite strange, to the second year vet student who takes three or four days to get the amount of sleep she should be getting each night, to hear someone claim that we "have it too easy." Part of this difference of opinion can be explained by differences in perspective; to the average veterinary student, the future is a question mark, yawing uncertainly into the future. That's why perfection is still seductive. It loudly calls our names, especially when we fail, telling us that if we only get another A, only impress another clinician, our future will precipitate into something a little more certain, into something a little safer.

From the faculty point of view, that students have it easy seems almost self-evident, even as the paradigm among veterinary students is to see their problems—stress, weight gain, setbacks, interpersonal drama—as a total function of their current situation, as a veterinary student. The orthodoxy among today's vet students claims that all of these terrible emotions we're feeling are somehow caused—engineered, maybe—by vet school and nothing else, and that upon graduation all of our stress and our problems will immediately evaporate like a bad dream. The faculty members undoubtedly hear this talking point, and want to (and sometimes do) tell us that we are failing to see that the particularities of our current problems are just instantiations of larger patterns that, unless corrected, will haunt us for the rest of our lives—namely, perfectionism.

Hendrix, as he mentions in the lecture, believes that experience teaches us that perfectionism is more likely to kill you than to save you.

Not that many people expect this gulf in opinion to be bridged anytime soon. In an essay for the *New Yorker*, Andrew Solomon said, "While all old people have been young, no young people have been old, and this troubling fact engenders the frustration of all parents and elders, which is that while you can describe your experience you cannot confer it" (Solomon, 2016).

So what is to be done? Having sat in on several teaching seminars, I understand the two camps of faculty members roughly to be: 1) make vet school less stressful by giving easier and less frequent exams, and by giving take-home assignments and/or extra credit assignments, or 2) tell the students, "No, you really *shouldn't* be stressed, can't you see? How are you going to handle taxes and marriages falling apart when you can't even handle a 5/10 on a weekly quiz?"

Of course these are caricatures of the two extremes, and there are valid points to be made by both sides. However, something that seems absent from the discussion is the role that honest conversation can play.

More often than not, during the first three years of our veterinary education, the student-professor relationship is limited to didactic lectures, and the result is an occasional failure to fully humanize each other, to appreciate each other's struggles as real and valid, to understand each other's stories.

And it's in this last point that I think the real genius of Dr. Hendrix's last lecture lies. The reason this talk resonated with so many is that it was a collection of honest stories. As he mentions in the lecture, the person that students saw behind the lecture podium for all those years was really just a character. The real Charlie Hendrix—a man who served in the military, a man who worries more than he likes to let on, a man who now carries Hot Wheel cars in his pockets for the moments when his grandson starts to cry—was only revealed through a conversation. He used his voice to tell his story and to become more human.

Our profession should do more of the same—make efforts to use our voices to tell the stories of ourselves and of each other in order to dig down to the less apparent truths that were hidden away.

As Solomon wrote later on in that same essay, "it is nearly impossible to hate anyone whose story you know." He used the word "hate," but I think his observation rings just as true when we replace "hate" with words like "judge," "condemn," or "fail to love."

Visitors to Auburn's College of Veterinary Medicine today will likely spend much of their time in one of the campus' two newest buildings: the VEC and the Small Animal Teaching Hospital. Perhaps either because of their ailing pet being treated in the latter, or their smiling son or daughter giving a case presentation in the former, these visitors may be forgiven for overlooking the squat, non-descript white concrete building that sits a literal stone's throw away from the newer buildings: Greene Hall, formerly the Basic Sciences Building and the location of many faculty offices and first- and second-year laboratories.

The observant individual will notice that to the left of the entrance to this building there's a bronze plaque with a smiling, cherubic face in bas-relief. The face is of course that of the building's namesake, Dr. James E. Greene, the fourth dean of the college.

Hendrix said, "We used to have a trivia competition for students, and there was a question that asked, 'What is the greatest legacy that Dr. Greene left behind?' The textbook answer to that, of course, is that he moved us out to Wire

Road. But one time, a group of students came to me and asked me 'Dr. Hendrix, what is the greatest legacy that Dr. Greene left behind?' and I told them my answer instead: Mrs. Greene."

He told me that a few years after her husband was appointed dean of the college, Mrs. Greene caught wind that the parents of Dr. LaVerne Krista[10] (who taught at Auburn's vet school from 1969 to 1998) were coming down from North Dakota for a visit. "She used to give tea, high tea, and when she heard about Dr. Krista's parents she wanted to invite them over."

With glee, Hendrix described everything from the china and silverware Mrs. Greene used, to the meal that she prepared for the Kristas' visit.

---

[10] Hendrix told me that in his thick North Dakota accent, Dr. Krista used to say to the students in the first-year histology course, "Das a macrophage, eyou gotta know dat one!"

"These were just a couple of simple farmers," Hendrix said, but in spite that fact, Mrs. Greene showed them an Auburn version of opulence that invited, rather than overwhelmed. "She had the ability to march right up to that line of ostentatious and stay on the correct side. She always knew how to do it."

Mrs. Greene's eye for the elegant was expansive, and included not only the opulent, but the simple as well. One May, shortly after he came to Auburn, Dr. Hendrix was sitting in church with his daughter when he saw a bouquet of sunflowers sitting on the altar. He looked in the program and found a note that said, "Flowers in memory of Lt. James E. Greene, Jr."

Some years prior, in May of 1969, the Greenes' son had been shot and killed at the age of 26 while heading a Navy riverboat patrol on the Saigon

River in Vietnam (Vietnam Veterans Memorial Fund, 1969). To memorialize him, Mrs. Greene was said to buy flowers each year on the anniversary of his death. "Just sunflowers," said Hendrix. "Nothing fancy. Sometimes less is more."

Over the years, in the hopes of keeping her spirits elevated, Dr. Hendrix would see Mrs. Greene on campus and would joke around with her, sometimes asking her when she was going to run for homecoming queen. Babe McGehee[11], the brother of Mrs. Greene, was grateful for these attempts. He told Hendrix, "You have no idea how much that means to my sister."

---

[11] On November 30, 1939, Coleman "Babe" McGehee scored the first touchdown in what would eventually be called Jordan-Hare Stadium. His wife, Suzelle, was the daughter of Cliff Hare, first president of the SEC and a namesake of the stadium. Babe passed away in 2005 at the age of 86 (Auburn Athletics, 2014).

Other faculty members offered their condolences as well. A wooden frame bearing the Lieutenant's name was assembled to hold a globe in his memory. When the frame fell into disrepair, Dr. Arvle Marshall[12] (Texas A&M, Class of 1964) attempted to repair its structure, but the plates that bore the Lieutenant's name, along with a short inscription, still needed to be replaced.

Hendrix said, "The brass had come off the plates, so I took them down to Ware Jewelers and asked them to duplicate them."

When he returned to pick up the finished product, they told him they had duplicated the plates, per his request, but had also made a

---

[12] Dr. Arvle E. Marshall taught Anatomy at Auburn for 23 years, and assembled many of the anatomical skeletal models that currently decorate the halls of Greene Hall. According to Dr. Hendrix, other faculty members would refer to him as "Arvle Knarvle," a play on the name of the famous stunt performer Evel Knievel, in reference to Dr. Marshall's motorcycle.

second set of plates. They asked Hendrix which set he thought looked better.

The globe still resides near the back of the vet school's library (named for the school's first dean, Charles Allen Cary (Iowa State University, Class of 1887)). Mounted on the wooden frame is the set that Hendrix chose—two small plates with silver serif lettering on what looks like blue metallic marble. The twin plates read[13]:

IN MEMORY OF JAMES E. GREENE, JR.
LT. U.S. NAVY
KILLED IN ACTION IN VIETNAM
MAY 11, 1969

PRESENTED BY SOUTH GEORGIA VMA
ALABAMA VMA
DR. W.G. WHITTICK
DR. AND MRS. J.M. WHITTEN

---

[13] Dr. William G. Whittick (Ontario Veterinary College, Class of 1955) was a Diplomate of the American College of Veterinary Surgeons, and wrote a textbook on canine orthopedics.

But for all the effort put into memorializing the life of her son and into recovering from the emotional trauma that occurs when a mother has to bury her child, the life of Mrs. Mary Greene and her myriad accomplishments[14] never had a chance to be likewise memorialized until 2012, in the last several years of her life.

With the newly-constructed Veterinary Education Center awaiting its first class of veterinary students, Hendrix and several other faculty members felt that something was lacking in the campus' newest additions.

"There are two magnolias out there in the turnaround," said Hendrix, twisting in his chair and gesturing toward the trees that were now

---

[14] After getting her master's from Syracuse University, Mary Greene became a clinical social worker, and made the *Who's Who of American Women* list in 1984. She went on to found the Auburn Service League (Harding, 2015).

illuminated only by the halogen lamps of the parking lot, since the sun had already set. "Two magnolia trees. That one on the left I bought. It's called the Mary Greene magnolia. The other one is the Jimmy Greene magnolia."

He turned back to me and laughed in spite of himself, saying wasn't it was funny how everything from the buildings to the bushes seemed to be named after somebody? "Even the trees have names around here," he said.

It can be argued that the central fact about Dr. Hendrix is his predilection for names, the skill he said he acquired from his mother and passed onto his daughter. This fact goes beyond mere trivia; it can expand our understanding of Charlie Hendrix the man, not the character.

For example, one of the things that Hendrix especially loved about Mrs. Greene is that she always said to him, "How's Charlotte?" rather than just "How's your daughter?" She called her by her name.

During our interview, when Hendrix would go down one of his manic story-telling rabbit holes, he'd frequently mention places and people whose names I had never heard. On the occasions when he noticed the blank look on my face, he'd laugh and say, "Son, you need to get out more."

Dr. Hendrix is a man who not only prefers but loves names and the rich textures they confer on our experience of life. This love—for the specific over the general, the personal over the stereotypical—could arguably explain his career choice as well.

Hendrix got his master's not because he had a passion for research but because he wanted to teach. But why parasitology? I can't think of another field in veterinary medicine where names are so central to its work. Part of his decision to choose parasitology, if not most, can obviously be explained by the influence of his mentor, Dr. Schlotthauer, who was a veterinary parasitologist. But it certainly couldn't have hurt that he chose a specialty where the seeing-naming reflex arc is so prevalent.

Hendrix is famous for telling his students to think: "how are things alike and how are they different?" Overlooking the comically obvious differences, here's what I see as the same: Dr. Hendrix spotting a student in the hall from years ago and shouting his name with exuberant familiarity, and Dr. Hendrix splashing a picture of the screwworm on the projector screen, shouting its scientific name with the same joy.

The idea that names matter is an easy pill to swallow in a place like Auburn, where every street and sidewalk and lamppost, it seems like, is plastered with the name of some person, maybe long-dead or maybe living, who has changed the face of this place in some way. Where, to echo Hendrix, even the trees have names.

Hendrix mentions in his lecture a student named Joseph Palmer (Class of 2014), who asked him, "Dr. Hendrix, what do you want to be when you grow up?" I believe that a knowledge of his infatuation with names takes us one step beyond that question, offering us a *why*, however incomplete, behind Joseph Palmer's *what*.

At the conclusion of the interview, as we were standing and trading small talk before going our separate ways, we were politely interrupted by a student who started engaging Dr. Hendrix in the type of idle banter at which he is a certified professional.

Before long he dove into one of his stories, which ended with him telling us that if he ever hits the Georgia lottery, we can bet there'll be a lot more scholarships to go around at this school.

The other student told him, "Just don't forget to buy something for yourself."

Once the other student had departed, Hendrix told me, through a smile, that students have been telling him that for years. Students used to jokingly refer to his disheveled and overstuffed office as Mary Poppins' purse, given its near-magical ability to contain more that its volume should physically allow (and to produce needed items on command).

Years ago, after the office had produced one such item for a student, the student echoed our present-day interlocutor by saying, "Don't forget to pull something out for yourself."

Luck being as fickle as it is, I'm not sure sudden and unexpected millions from the Georgia lottery are an issue Dr. Hendrix will ever have to face. But in the absence of such fortune, I have something a little more modest to offer.

To Dr. Hendrix, and to every other teacher who has made the dreams of their students (including me) seem a little less remote: this one's for you.

◉

A Last Lecture

Dr. Charles Hendrix
Feb. 11, 2016

[*Over a packed Overton Auditorium, a song plays—"Last Dance" by Donna Summer. To cheers and hollers, a figure appears in the door at the rear of the room. Wire-haired and bespectacled, Dr. Charlie Hendrix dances his way down the steps. He waits for the applause to die down at the conclusion of the music and asks everyone to please have a seat.*]

Ladies and gentlemen, I don't know if you know this or not, but that was "Last Dance" by the beautiful Donna Summer. It is the song that traditionally marks the death of disco[15]. I

---

[15] "Last Dance" by Donna Summer (aka the Queen of Disco) was a song from the 1978 movie *Thank God It's Friday*. It went on to win the Academy Award for Best

used that song because "Take This Job and Shove It," was just not appropriate tonight.

[*Audience laughs*]

It was a close runner-up. [*Smiling*] Only kidding.

I have been here at Auburn for 34 years and 7 months, and what I want to tell you about tonight is all the mistakes I've made and all the things I've learned. We're gonna make this fun, but there will be some serious parts.

First of all, the inspiration for this lecture came from a man by the name of Randy Pausch, who taught at Carnegie Mellon in Pittsburgh. He was a professor and famous computer engineer, and tragically, he was only 45 years old when he came

---

Original Song, as well as a Grammy Award for Best Female R&B Performance. The following year, in July of 1979, saw the death of disco, and consequently, this song is often cited as the last great disco hit. (Roberts, 2006)

down with pancreatic cancer. And he gave the last lecture of his life to all his students and friends. Now, I'm not dying, I'm just retiring, but if you get a chance, I want you to go to YouTube and watch his lecture[16]. It is riveting.

The next thing I want to tell you is that when you start veterinary school, Dr. Givens and Liesl talk to you a lot about personalities and personality types. There's something called the Meyers-Briggs Personality Test. If you've never taken it, I want you to take it and find out exactly who you

---

[16] The lecture, titled "Really Achieving Your Childhood Dreams," was given on September 18, 2007, almost one year after Pausch's diagnosis of pancreatic cancer and eight months before his death, to hundreds of friends, students and fellow faculty at Carnegie Mellon University. The lecture was viewed millions of times online, and was eventually converted into a book called *The Last Lecture*, which sat on the New York Times' best-seller list for 80 straight weeks. My hopes for this tome are slightly more modest. (The New York Times, 2008)

are, because once you find out who you are, you are really enlightened.

Now me, when I take it, I am an ENFP. That stands for Extroverted, Intuitive, Feeling and Perceptive. The type of people who are ENFPs include: Snoopy the Dog, Robin Williams, Mark Twain, Maria von Trapp from *The Sound of Music* [*laughter*]. One of the things about ENFPs, though, is—well I'll tell you some other ENFPs: Che Guevara and Fidel Castro are ENFPs. Muammar Gaddafi is an ENFP. So it's not always nice people, but I'm proud to be an ENFP.

The opposite of an ENFP is something called an ISTJ: Introverted, Subjective, Thinking, Judgmental individuals. These are the true leaders of our country. Dwight D. Eisenhower, the leader of D-Day and president of the United

States. George Washington, they were both ISTJs.

Now, I'm the complete opposite of Dwight Eisenhower. If we were storming the beaches of Normandy, Eisenhower would be leading the men into battle, and I would be serving donuts and coffee [*laughter*]. That's how it works. I wanted to get that point across.

I also want to introduce my lovely wife of 43 years, Becky. She's sitting over there. My lovely daughter Charlotte, who's also joined us tonight. My son-in-law (who is a Kentuckian) is not here. He is with my grandson, Charlie. Charlie is unfortunately having a bad night tonight and wasn't able to make it.

A Bit about Me

Courtesy of Charles M. Hendrix

Ladies, and gentlemen, right off the bat: I'm from Greenville, South Carolina. I graduated from Greenville High. I left the county, which was both wonderful and unexpected. I went to Clemson for three years. I spent four years at the University of Georgia's College of Veterinary Medicine. For that reason, I will say that I am a Georgia boy, but I am an Auburn man.

So that's my education. Now, little known facts about me. When I was thirteen years old, I invented a super hero for DC comics, no kidding. Her name is Gas Girl. When you're thirteen years old, all you're ever doing is thinking about gas [*laughter*]. I won the contest. I was thirteen years old, just starting the ninth grade. Big time.

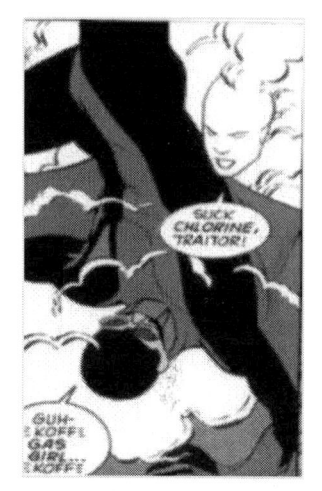

DC Comics

Now let me tell you something about Gas Girl: she has made 23 appearances in DC comics and I have yet to see a dime from her [*laughter*].

So if you don't believe me, here comes a cover of my comic book.

62   The Trees Have Names

DC Comics

Over here is sitting my radiation oncologist, Dr. Cabelka[17]. Now doc, I bet you never knew that about your patient.

[*The doctor responds, "I did not."*]

Next thing: when I lived in Minnesota, I won a house for one dollar! They were raffling off houses for one dollar in the inner city of Minneapolis to get young people to move back. I bought this house pictured here for one dollar, no kidding. I wound up selling it for $55,000. I recently got online to look into it, and it's listed at $255,000 these days.

I should've kept it [*laughter*].

There's my little daughter in the snow, and there's my 1940 Chevy.

---

[17] Of Cabelka's last name, Hendrix remarked, "I think it's Czech. It means little tiny jewel purse."

Other little known facts. [*A video of dancing beings to play. Music by Frank Sinatra is on in the background.*] Two years ago I was one of the dancing stars of east Alabama. They asked who I wanted for a partner, and I said, "Give me Ginger Rodgers!" [18]

Do y'all know who that is? Fred Astaire's partner?[19] Ah, never mind.

---

[18] Fred Astaire and Ginger Rogers were a dance couple who appeared in 10 films in the 1930s and 40s. Astaire, who got his start as a Vaudeville child actor at the turn of the century, first teamed up with Rogers in the 1933 film *Flying Down to Rio*. The pair won an Academy Award the following year, for Best Original Song. (Biography, 2015)

[19] In an interview with Auburn University's PR service, *Wire Eagle*, Hendrix said, "Everybody knows that Ginger Rogers did all the dances that Fred Astaire danced, but she danced them backwards and in high heels. I can dance all of the dances that Katherine Hoerlein dances, but I can dance them with the results of four rotator cuff surgeries and with an artificial left hip." (Hohenstatt, 2014)

Courtesy of Charles M. Hendrix

Well, *my* Ginger Rodgers was Dr. Benjamin F. Hoerlein's granddaughter. Hoerlein as in Hoerlein Hall[20]. We were Team Vet Med! Before the show, there was a guy who was a body builder, lifting people up and twirling them around. Of course, I don't have any shoulders. But there was

---

[20] Constructed in 1970 and dedicated in '71, Hoerlein Hall was used as Auburn's small animal hospital until the construction of Bailey Small Animal Teaching Hospital in 2014. The building was named for Benjamin F. Hoerlein, veterinary neurologist by training, professor of Small Animal Surgery & Medicine, and founder and inaugural director of the Scott-Ritchey Research Center. (Weaver, 2008)

this guy, when we were in the dressing room before the show, and he looked at me and said, "I'm gonna be ripping my clothes off—what are you gonna do?"

I said to him, "I'll be twirling a parasol!" [*laughter*]

So I had us penciled us in for last place. We were gonna lose, I figured. Big time. What I didn't know was that we would wind up winning the Audience Choice Award.

Now let me tell you this: [*pulling out a trophy*] this is not how I operate. These days, when you win a trophy, the trophy is made out of plastic. Ladies and gentlemen, never ever give someone a plastic trophy. It doesn't *mean* anything.

If they give you a plastic trophy, you get on the Internet, you find a real metal trophy, you buy it for yourself, and have it engraved. [*He pulls out a different trophy, a metal one, and holds it up]* Just like this. [*Audience cheers*]

[*After a moment, looking at the trophy and tilting it in the light*] I don't think my wife and daughter ever knew I bought this.

Don't laugh; there's much more tonight to come.

Now, there's a point to this. That night, Katherine Hoerlein, the most important thing she said to me that night, right before we went on, was, "If anything goes wrong, you just keep smiling. No one will ever know."

And that's one of the secrets of life. When something goes wrong, you keep smiling and no one will ever know. Write that down.

Hit the next slide, Emily.

THE RHYTHM OF LIFE

Courtesy of Charles M. Hendrix

[The audience cheers and hollers as the image appears on the screen.]

Woo, I love to swim. I have been swimming at least one mile every day since September 1974. From '94 to '97, I entered a competition to see how far I could swim in the month of February. The first year I was first in my age group, third in the world. Second year I was first in my age group, third in the world. Third year I was first in my age group, *second* in the world.

And then finally, in my fourth year, I was first in my age group, first in the world.

Now, there are 28 days in February (29 days in '96). How far do you think I swam? Give me a number.

[*Audience member shouts "250!"*] No, more.

[*"300!"*] More.

Courtesy of Charles M. Hendrix

[*"350!"*] A little more than that. 358.01 miles was how far I swam. And that picture is me after I finished. That fellow on the left is Auburn's own Rowdy Gaines.[21] If you don't know who Rowdy Gaines is, he is the fellow who gets excited when the Lithuanian guy wins in the Olympics. He doesn't care where they're from, he just likes swimming.

This next picture was taken in 2006, in Idaho.

---

[21] Rowdy Gaines is a former competitive swimmer, first for Auburn University (1977-1981), then for the U.S. Olympic team in the 1984 Summer Olympics in Los Angeles, California, where he won three gold medals: 100 meter freestyle, 4x100-meter freestyle relay, 4x100-meter medley relay. In 1991, Gaines became afflicted with the autoimmune condition Guillain-Barré Syndrome, in which peripheral nerves are attacked by the immune system, resulting in paralysis. Gaines eventually made a (surprising) full recovery and went on to become the oldest person to qualify for the 1996 Summer Olympics, although he ultimately decided not to participate. He set ten world records during his swimming career. (Sports Reference, n.d.) (Auburn University, 2007)

Courtesy of Charles M. Hendrix

[*Staring for a moment, then turning to the audience*] I am one good-looking specimen.

I had a student put this photograph on HotOrNot.com on the Over 50 category and I received a rating of 8.5 [*applause*].

Now, obviously I don't look like that anymore. People say to me, Dr. Hendrix, what happened? Well let me tell you, and this is important so write this down: it's the rhythm of life. I got old. And it's gonna happen to everybody. I'll talk a little bit about that later...but *god* I was handsome [*laughter*].

Back in 1997, I could sell aluminum siding to someone who lived in an igloo, let me tell you. They asked me to give a motivational speech to the men's and women's swimming and diving team when they came back from the Olympics. And when they came back, the men went on to win a bona fide national championship. Now, I don't count that 1957 thing[22] because we put the crown on ourselves, but this was the first national championship—in any sport—that we won on our own. This is one for the books. I don't know if you realize this but growing up, I was the fat kid who

---

[22] Since 1998, the championship for NCAA college football has been (unofficially) determined by a championship game between the top two teams (or top four since 2014), as determined by an AP poll. In 1957, when Auburn claims to have won a national championship, the champion was understood to be the top-ranked team at the conclusion of the season. No actual championship game was played in those days. (McCarter, 2011)

always got picked last in gym class. And now, I have an NCAA ring for giving that speech. I never thought I'd do this. My friend Rick Theobald showed me how to shake hands if you have a national championship ring.

[*Dr. Hendrix extends his hand to an audience member, who shakes it. Hendrix pronates his hand such that the ring is shining in the face of the audience member.*] Charlie Hendrix, nice to meet you! [*Audience roars with laughter.*]

Now, I only break the ring out if I don't feel good about myself...or if we have an SEC football game.

The Bucket List

One of the things in life I love is *Antique Roadshow*, and it was always my dream to be on *Antique Roadshow*, so when it came to

Birmingham, I got tickets, okay? And so, I'm on the right hand portion of the screen. You'll see me carrying a very large picture. Hit it, Emily.

[*Video plays. Screaming, laughter, applause*]

See me walking by? I was on *Antique Roadshow*!

Public Broadcasting Service

Let me tell you something, ladies and gentlemen, let me tell you something that my wife doesn't know: I'm gonna get on *Antique Roadshow* again, and this time I'm gonna get on the film. Let me very quickly explain.

To get on *Antique Roadshow*, you have to have some rich relative who went somewhere and found something or bought something, some nice souvenir, and then they gave it to you. *Or*, you have to be real lucky at the Goodwill. When you're on *Antique Roadshow*, you gotta have back story, you gotta have papers.

Let me tell you: I went to the Goodwill, and for 50 cents I found a piece of pottery that said "Tuskegee Institute Pottery."

In the old days, if you wanted something done right, you went to the Tuskegee Institute. They had the finest tailors, upholsterers, potters, you name it. And it turns out, they had a fine ceramics department down there, too. Headed by a man named Isaac Scott Hathaway who taught the students how to make pottery, and they used to sell this stuff.

How much pottery is down at Tuskegee today? Anyone know?

The answer is, they have nothing.

How much pottery do we have at the Jule Collins Smith Museum of Fine Art?

There is one piece. Because I gave it to them. They didn't have anything. But I want to tell you about Isaac Scott Hathaway.

He was invited to come to Auburn in 1948 to teach young white girls pottery in the school of home economics. He was the first African American to ever teach here at Auburn, in 1948. Do you know how much trouble we had with people objecting to that? I've put all the headlines up there on the screen. [*A blank slide appears*] It was nothing. We just did it.

And what I have done, is gotten online and found pieces of Isaac Scott Hathaway's pottery. So far, I have bought about eight pieces.

Becky, don't get mad at me. It could be worse; it could be a boat [*laughter*]. So that's my plan to get back on *Antique Roadshow*.

INFLUENCE ON TEACHING

This lady right here is a lady by the name of Mary Wiles. All of my students know, I'm always telling you, "We have got to know how to think. How are things alike and how are they different?

Courtesy of Charles M. Hendrix

That's all that life is, if you want to learn something."

Mary Wiles was the one who taught me to think that way. She was a wonderful teacher.

Now, as you might be able to tell from her lips, she wore dentures. And these dentures were *loose*. And when she laughed, they would clack, so it was my goal in life to get her to laugh.

Consequently, she was very tight-lipped around me. Very wonderful woman.

The next topic coming up, I've got to do a little bit of backstory on. [*Dr. Hendrix takes a long drink of sweet tea from Mike and Ed's Barbecue.*] I want you to know where this character of Charlie Hendrix came from, as a teacher.

There's a place called Hilton Head in South Carolina, real ritzy place. Everyone who's anyone goes there. But there's an island right next to it called Daufuskie Island. You've gotta get there by ferry. There's no bridge there.

In 1969 it was one of the poorest places on Earth. They had no teachers there. And there was a man by the name of Pat Conroy who went there, a famous South Carolinian author who wrote *The Water is Wide*, *The Prince of Tides*, *The Great Santini*, and *Beach Music*. Lots of books about the low country of South Carolina.

What happened was, he became a school teacher in the Beaufort County school system. He went to teach these kids on the island.

He would walk up to one of these kids, who had never been taught anything, and he'd hold up three fingers and say, "Sugar, how many fingers am I holding up?" And she would say "Two?"

They weren't taught anything, so he had the challenge of becoming their teacher.

Now, this particular book, called *The Water is Wide*, appeared as a movie called *Conrak*, starring Jon Voight, Angelina Jolie's father. This movie was made in the early 1970s. It was this movie that made me want to become a teacher in the first place.

So, I'm gonna show you where the persona, this Charlie Hendrix that you see up in the parasitology lab—this mad man, this crazy man—I'm going to show you where he came from. Emily, I think this is it.

[*A video clip plays*]

> *"I want y'all to take a real long look at me. Shouldn't be any hardship, 'cause I'm handsome. A thousand years of Irish inbreeding have produced these fine*

features: this pug nose, this pugnacious jaw. Moreover, I have a penetrating wit, a fanciful imagination, and my eyes are almost as blue as Paul Newman's. I am your teacher."

[*Laughing*] He is crazy. He is crazy as a loon.

Now in this next clip, a young girl is about to tell Jon Voight that she's to become the wife of an older man. What's gonna happen is that he's going to explode at the fact that this 13 year old is going to be marrying an old man. He's going to say some things, and give her what he expects of her. He's gonna mention some role models.

He'll mention Wanda Landowska, who was a Polish harpsichordist who escaped Hitler. She read Bach's music like Bach wrote it. When she played the harpsichord it sounded like a brand new Singer sewing machine. It was great. He's gonna talk about her.

He's gonna talk about Marian Anderson. Marian Anderson was a contra alto who was supposed to sing at Constitution Hall, but the Daughters of the American Revolution said because she was black, she couldn't sing there. Now, it's February, which is black history month. Well, Eleanor Roosevelt fixed it up so Marian ended up singing at the Lincoln Memorial instead, on Easter Sunday. It looked like MLK was speaking. There were people everywhere. She sang, "My Country Tis of Thee."

The third person he mentions is someone by the name of Mary McLeod Bethune, a black educator who founded Bethune-Cookman College in Daytona Beach, Florida. She was a confidant, a counselor to FDR. She was invited to the White House to confer with the president. She got to the gate, and in the olden times, sometimes people could be disrespectful. An older black gentleman was referred to as "uncle," and an older black woman was referred to as "auntie." Obviously that's not right, but it's the way things were. I'm just telling you the way things were.

So the guard asked her, "What are you doing here, auntie?"

She said, "I'm here to confer with the president." Then after a moment, she said, "By the way, which one of my sisters' children are you?" [*Laughter*]

Finally, let me tell you what she did (and you need to write this down, because this is important). She told Eleanor Roosevelt: "No one can ever make you feel inferior without your consent." Don't you ever forget that. If someone ever makes you feel bad about yourself, the only way they'll be successful is if you let them do it.

Don't you let them do it.

Ms. Mary McLeod had a hard life, but she taught Eleanor that. Roll it, Emily.

[*A second video clip plays*]

> *"They gonna get my daddy a new plough. Fix up my brother's teeth."*
>
> *"What's he gonna do for you?"*
>
> *"He'll get me a new red dress."*
>
> *"He'd be getting you pretty cheap."*
>
> *"Ain't no business of yours, no how."*
>
> *"Alright go ahead, throw your books in the river. Go back to counting on your fingers. Have fourteen kids in a row,*

look sixty when you're thirty. Let your brain rot in your skull."

"Why do you always pick on me?"

"Because The Gospel According to Conrak is our will. Higher, stronger, faster, better. Not a floor scrubber but Wanda Landowska. Not a diaper changer but Marian Anderson. Not a pig slopper but Mary McLeod the Third. Not a fry cook but Eleanor Roosevelt. Either a Caesar or nobody."

Hit the next slide.

One more movie. There is a movie that came out thirty years ago called *Out of Africa*. I don't know if you've ever seen it, but it is both a guy movie and a chick flick.

Meryl Streep plays Baroness Karen von Blixen. Robert Redford plays Denys Finch Hatton. They lived in Kenya around the time of the First World War. Robert Redford was a big game hunter who came to realize that certain things—this big game hunting and the things we were doing to the environment—just weren't right, and he came to change his ways.

He died in a plane crash. The Baroness had to bury him, and then she had to go back to Denmark because all of her money was gone. You're going hear her words. She says, "The district commissioner reports that lions have found Finch Hatton's grave. They've leveled it off to a platform so that they can look at the wildlife below." And then she says, "Dennis would be so pleased." What's cut out of this clip is, "I must tell him when I see him."

The reason I'm using this is, I trained at the University of Minnesota, under a fellow up there named John C. Schlotthauer[23]. This was my mentor. You saw the bluster of Conrak. Well, this man was the parasitologist who trained me. And he said some things to me that changed my life.

He once told me, "I love you almost as much as I love my own sons."

Do you know what that did to me?

He treated me wonderfully. I didn't have any ideas in my head about research or parasitology, but he got me started. I'm good to you because he

---

[23] Dr. John C. Schlotthauer was a veterinary parasitologist who graduated from the University of Minnesota's veterinary college. Both his father and his brother were veterinarians. Interestingly, his father, Carl F. Schlotthauer (1893-1959), was the first laboratory animal veterinarian in the U.S. (Anderson, 2015)

was good to me. He primed the pump, and for that I loved him very much.

[*A long pause*] He died of multiple myeloma. When he first got the diagnosis, I called up a physician friend of mine, and I said, "Tell me everything you know about multiple myeloma."

And the first thing he said, you could almost hear the smile coming out of the phone. He said, "You know what? Only the best people get that one."

And we see that in veterinary medicine. The sweetest dog gets demodicosis. The best cat is the one that comes down with a mammary tumor. It only happens to the best ones.

He died in 1992, and the students at Minnesota lamented. Outside of his office, what they did was they pulled up this big rock and they put a plaque on it, and they stood back, and they said, "It's not good enough. Let's plant a tree."

Courtesy of Charles M. Hendrix

So they planted the most beautiful golden maple. And in the fall of every year, it turns the most beautiful golden color you ever saw.

John would be so pleased. I must remember to tell him.

WHEN YOU FALL

Alright ladies and gentlemen, now we're getting into the meat of the lecture, [*checking watch*] and I hope we're not going to go too long on this one, but it's important that I tell you this. When you graduate from vet school, you think that your problems are solved. You think there's gonna be rainbows, don't you? And unicorns! [*laughter*] And everything is going to be perfect because you've reached your goal in life. Right?

I'm here to tell you that that is not true. Life goes *pfft pfft* real quick. I'm always saying that.

The important thing to learn here, something that scares me about this generation, is there's so much emphasis on perfection.

You don't have to be perfect when you're learning veterinary medicine, you just have to get a B! A little later on, you'll learn that perfection can kill you. Conrak wasn't asking for perfection, he was asking her, or he was trying, to give her a voice. That's why you came to college: to gain a voice. If you see something wrong, say something. This isn't about perfection at all.

From the book of James, chapter 1, verses 2 through 8 (and this is the important part):

> *"My brethren, count it all joy when you fall into various trials, knowing that the testing of your faith produces patience. But let patience have its perfect work. That you may be perfect and complete, lacking nothing. If any of you lacks wisdom, let him ask of God, who gives to all liberally and without reproach, and it will be given to him. But let him ask in faith, with no doubting, for he who doubts is like a wave of the sea, driven and tossed by the wind. For let not that man suppose that he will receive*

> *anything from the Lord; he is a double-minded man, unstable in all his ways."*

Notice that this doesn't say *if* you fall into trials, it says, *when* you fall into trials.

Things are going to happen to you. And you are going to need a way to get out of it. "If any of you lacks wisdom, let him ask of God who gives to all liberally and without reproach."

Remember that.

Next slide, Emily.

THE ELEPHANTS IN THE ROOM

In his last lecture, Randy Pausch talked about his cancer. I'm gonna talk about two things that are very important to me.

The first thing is, thirty years ago, I came down with a very bad case of clinical depression. It was awful. I did not know what was wrong with me. Let me tell you how it felt. The best way I found to describe it to someone is that it was like taking your hand and pressing it to a hinge on the gates of hell.

And that's why I've got this picture up here. Do you know how hard it is to find a picture on Google images of the gates of hell? [*laughter*] It is awful. It is hard because there are a lot of naked people. So I couldn't—[*Dr. Hendrix joining the audience in laughter*] I mean, this man is only half-naked.

But anyway, not to make light of this. As I was saying, I came down with a bad case of clinical depression. I didn't know what was wrong with me.

And I'm not trivializing this. Clinical depression, let me just say, is the common cold of mental illness. About 10% of people in this country have clinical depression. I'm not making light of it. Happens in women more than men. But it does happen. And it happened to me.

[*Another long pause*] I won teacher of the year. It was Dr. Johnson's class that nominated me. And what happened was, I got it in my head that everything had to be *perfect*. It had to be perfect. And if it wasn't perfect when I was teaching, I was wrong. I turned anger in on myself. It was awful.

That's what depression is: it's just anger turned inward. And I'm not trivializing here, I'm trying to help people understand. I was six months going into this depression, I was six months coming out. Dr. Joe Newton stood by me. My wife stood by me. A lady by the name of Glenda Bufford stood by me.

And I did a lot of praying. I made a deal with God, even. I said, "You get me out of this, and I will always be there for someone with clinical depression. I will always be there to share this with someone who has what I have. I promise you that, I promise I will." I prayed and prayed and prayed.

My father stood by me, too. I remember being in New Orleans sometime that year and calling him up and saying, "Dad, I feel like garbage."

My dad said, "Son, God does not make garbage." And that's the truth. God doesn't make garbage. We're all beautiful creatures.

Here's the secret, if you're suffering from clinical depression, here's the key: you have to find something beautiful that you can hold onto. I had to find something beautiful about myself. I had to find something unique about myself, something I could love.

And it turns out that I've got eyes that are bluer than Paul Newman's.

That's where I started, and I went from there. And I prayed. I prayed and I prayed and I prayed and I prayed. To the young women involved in the Christian Veterinary Fellowship, I said, "I gotta get this out and it's gotta be done right."

On October the 11th, 1984 I felt it. I woke up in the middle of the night, and everything came together. It all congealed. I felt the Holy Spirit healing me, and all day long I was on this tremendous high. It all came back together. I understood how to fight this.

Twelve hours I had that feeling, and then that spirit left me. What does it feel like when that happens? It feels like you've been on a Delta airline jet and you've had a bad bump. But it was gone; I was healed.

Glenda Bufford gave me a verse to claim. And I've got it here [*pulling a piece of paper from his pocket*]. I feel like Sally Field as Norma Rae.[24] It says, "I can do all things through Christ who strengthens me.[25]" And I claimed that verse. That's what I did. I did it without a psychologist. I owe it all to a higher power.

Ladies and gentlemen, if you ever get in that condition, through perfection or something else, go for this verse. I know you're out there.

---

[24] Sally Field is an actress who played Norma Rae, the titular character in a 1979 movie based on the life of Crystal Lee Sutton, a woman from North Carolina who led a labor movement to unionize the textile factory in her hometown of Roanoke Rapids.
[25] Philippians 4:13, New King James Version

[*Looking at the paper again*] A little girl by the name of Marsha gave this to me. She said, "Dr. Hendrix, this is the verse that the psychologist used to bring *me* out."

I just want to let you know that. Depression is the elephant in the room, but I've got to talk about it.

Any questions? Then we'll move on.

Another elephant in the room: I won the cancer lottery! Back in 2012, I found out that I had prostate cancer. Let me get a slurp of tea real quick.

Gentlemen if you're sleeping, I need you to wake up. There are two types of men on God's green earth: those who have prostate problems, and those who are going to get prostate problems [*laughter*]. I came down with prostate cancer. Becky and I went up to Birmingham to see Scott Tully, a surgeon up there. He's got a machine that'll do the surgery on you, and one of the questions I had for him was, "You know when I'm running off papers sometimes and my Xerox machine is having a bad day? What do you when your robotic surgeon is having a bad day? With the Xerox machine, we just have jammed papers."

He says, "We'll cut you open and do it manually…or, we'll wait for another day." After that, he says, "We're gonna do the surgery in the morning, and we're going to catheterize you, and the next day you're going to have a bag strapped to your leg, and you're gonna go back to Auburn, and—"

I interrupted him and said, "I don't think so." I decided I was gonna have radiation therapy instead, and that's where I met my new best friend, Dr. Cabelka. He works at EAMC and he is truly my new best friend.

He's an ENFP. When we're around each other, I feel like I'm ten years old and I've got my best friend over for a sleepover. We're laughing, somebody farts, we're laughing some more [*audience laughs*].

And the tears! We laugh 'til the tears come down. Every time I see him, we have *fun*! I did 38 treatments with him. It was 38, wasn't it?

[*Dr. Cabelka says, "It was 44."*]

Forty-four treatments! And on that last treatment...well, men let me tell you real quick: when you have radiation therapy, you go in, you drop your drawers, you drop your underwear. They quickly throw the towel over, and you get—*Thip, thip, thip, thip, thip, thip*—you get radiated every day for like seven weeks.

But you finally finish. And the day I finished, I put on my tuxedo, and I went in. I had 44 roses for all the technicians. I even gave roses to a man! He came in when I dropped my drawers. And I was wearing my speedo with WAR EAGLE on the butt [*laughter*].

By the way, I look good in it.

Human medicine is different from veterinary medicine. When we castrate a horse, the farmer will say to you: "Doctor, I've put a bottle of Jack Daniels behind the seat of your car." You can't do that in human medicine! And I looked this up, ethically, and the reason you can't do that is, if I give Dr. Cabelka a bottle of liquor, that equates my life with a bottle of liquor.

I am worth more than a bottle of liquor!

So what they said was, a nice card from the Hallmark store will do. But I like to put thought into my gifts. When you give a gift, it's not about the gift, it's about the giver [*takes another drink of tea*]. I always give a gift on my anniversary of finishing radiation therapy. The first year, I gave him a book called, *Medicine, Magic, and Mystery*.[26] It was from 1938. The E.R. Squibb Company. It had the original presentation card in it from 1938. You can find anything on the Internet. And I also found a book called *Radiation Cookery* because he fried my insides! Which one do you think he liked better? That's right, *Radiation Cookery*.

---

[26] Dr. Howard W. Haggard, who wrote *Medicine, Magic, and Mystery* (plus dozens of other volumes on human medicine and its history) graduated from Yale's medical school in 1917. After serving in the Army Chemical Warfare Service in World War I, he returned to his alma mater and conducted physiological research that eventually led to "improvements in anesthesia and the development of the modern gas mask." Following the success of his 1929 book *Devils, Drugs, and Doctors* (he had an affinity for alliteration), Haggard spent the later part of his career splitting his time between research and science communication via books, public addresses, and radio broadcasts. (Rutgers University Center of Alcohol Studies, n.d.)

As I said before, when you give a trophy, you never give them plastic. Dr. Cabelka loves to play tennis, and so the next year, I got online and found this vintage tennis trophy. I had it all fixed up, it was beautiful.

On it, I had engraved, "World's Greatest Radiation Oncologist." Dr. Cabelka, where is that trophy?

[*"It's in my office."*]

It's in his office.

But where am I going with this? Oh yes, I won the cancer lottery. I want you to be very cognizant of cancer. All it takes is one cell going catawampus on you, in one organ.

Young women: know your bodies, okay? Thorough checkups, that kind of thing. I wanna stay politically correct. There's other stuff you need to do, but I can't say it here [*laughter*]. You know what I mean.

This cancer, it's bad stuff, okay? I got off easy. I won the cancer lottery, but I could have been very unlucky. There's people in this college who have been very unlucky, but I've been very lucky.

So that's the second elephant in the room.

What I Thought I Wanted

Ladies and gentlemen, I always wanted to be an Associate Dean of Academic Affairs. I'm not coveting, I am *not* coveting. I just always wanted to try this.

I thought to myself, I'd like to do that. So I went out on interviews. I put my name in the hat. I got turned down here at Auburn like three or four times. I went to Virginia, I went to Oklahoma, and

I went to Florida. I even went back to Georgia! Got turned down at all of them. I was the top man in the competition at Georgia...because all the other candidates were women [*laughter*].

But it never happened for me. It just never happened. So I just cut that out of my book. You know why? Because it really didn't matter.

One of the things I'm always doing is I'm always going up to students—and for thirty years I'd do this—I'd go up to them and say, "What do you want to do with your life?" and they would tell me. But no one ever asked *me* what *I* wanted to do with my life! For thirty years, no one ever asked me that question.

Until I met a kid by the name of Joseph Palmer. I said, "Joseph, what do you want to do with your life?" and Joseph gave me his answer. Then he goes, "Well Dr. Hendrix, what did *you* want to do?"

I said, "I've been waiting thirty years for someone to ask me that."

I wanted to be an Associate Dean for Academic Affairs, but it never happened, so I just cut it out of the book. And this is where sometimes the students are wiser than the teacher. Joseph said to me, "You wouldn't have liked that. That job's not for you. You're always in the hall yelling at us, and playing with us, things like that." He says, "You would've been miserable!"

And this is where I want you to understand: sometimes, y'all get so upset when someone says no to you. "I'm applying for this internship...[*imitating Eeyore's voice*] but I didn't get it." [*Audience laughs, impersonation continues*]: "I didn't...get it. My life is over!"

Ladies and gentlemen, let me tell you something. I have this on very good authority: "no" is a better answer than "yes." "No" will change your life like you will never believe. I wanted to go to University of Georgia, to their parasitology department. They told me no. I went to Minnesota instead, and I had the time of my life— I won a house, I got a baby, I had a wonderful time. It changed my life. And if I hadn't gone to Minnesota, I wouldn't be here at Auburn.

This is next slide is some wisdom I wanted to share with y'all. This is a man by the name of Garrison Keillor[27], in the Prairie Home Companion: "Some luck lies in not getting what you *thought* you wanted, but in getting what you

---

[27] Garrison Keillor is a writer who founded *A Prairie Home Companion*, an innovative and award-winning Minnesota public radio show that ran from 1974-2016. He now owns an independent bookstore in St. Paul Minnesota.

have, which once you have it, you may be smart enough to know that is what you would have wanted, had you known." That's a wise statement.

So when y'all don't get something, when they tell you no, that's fantastic. Don't worry about the yes. Look in the possibility of no.

[Dr. Hendrix takes another drink of tea as the slide changes.]

I Guess I Taught Her a Little Too Well

I get in some of the stickiest situations just by doing nothing. No good deed goes unpunished. And I've got one last story about it.

Ladies and gentlemen, we have a classroom without walls. Once I cover a topic with you, you have to remember that for the rest of your life. I taught Dr. Johnson during the 1983-'84 academic year.

Now, when y'all are in the halls with us and there's no administrator or bigwig or guest, there's something I like to do. Dr. Johnson, would you please stand up? You've got to do this. Are you ready?

[*Impersonating a drill sergeant*]: I taught you during the 1983-84 year! Of the information we covered back then, that year, what are you responsible for?

[*Dean Johnson responds, coolly*: *"All of it."*]

All of it! That's right! What is the scientific name for the lung fluke? [28]

---

[28] Flukes, also known as flatworms, are internal parasites that affect all veterinary species. Most have a complex life cycle, which means that the fluke must somehow pass through an intermediate host. In the case of *Paragonimus kellicotti*, which can cause a

[*"Paragonimus kellicotti."*]

There's one more question, and it's not what you think it's gonna be: how do you know that?

[*"Because I'm a veterinarian."*]

Courtesy of Wikipedia Commons

You can move along! [*Audience cheers*] Ladies and gentlemen, this is not a learn-and-flush profession. You've got to remember this stuff.

---

bloody sputum and persistent cough in dogs and cats, the intermediate host is a snail. (Taylor, 2015)

These two men on the screen are Laurel and Hardy[29]. They were slapstick comedians of silent movies, and also the early talkies. The fat one would always say to the thin one, "Another fine mess you've gotten us into here." So I'm gonna tell you my latest fine mess...you don't even know about this one, Dr. Johnson.

The title of this story is "I Guess I Taught Her a Little Too Well." Just last week I was giving a tour to some guests of ours who are interviewing for veterinary school. I had like forty people on a tour. Now, when I have people on a tour, Dr. Johnson calls me The Closer. I'm just like Michelle Obama[30]. I will close the deal in a minute.

---

[29] Englishman Stan Laurel and American Oliver Hardy were a slapstick duo and that performed together for nearly three decades. (McCabe, 1965)
[30] "The Closer" is a nickname that was given to Michelle Obama during her husband's 2008 presidential campaign after his political advisers noticed her

So I had forty people with me, and we had seen Greene Hall. We'd gone through a portion of the large animal clinic. And I pull them out...you know the big seal of Auburn's College of Veterinary Medicine that's out in the front lobby? I had people circled around that. And in that group was an alumna, a young woman from the class of 1999. And I'm showing off, thinking I'm gonna show these people how well I taught here, and so I asked her, with big seal on the floor between us, "There's the serpent on the stick, the *caduceus*, the staff of Asclepius. Do you know what parasite that signifies?"

And everybody here knows the name is...what?

---

unusually high conversion rate—the percentage of voters who agreed to help the campaign after Mrs. Obama appealed to them. (Davis, 2016)

[*Audience responds in unison: "Dracunculus insignis[31]"*]

[*Smiling*] ...Damn, I'm good. [*Audience laughs*]

So anyway, she answers correctly, and I said to myself, "Yes, I did it."

And then she said, "I even have it tattooed right back here!" And she raises her shirt, and sure enough she's got a tramp stamp!

I say, that's too much information!

Honest to God, it happened like that. I guess I taught her a little too well.

---

[31] The veterinary parasite *D. insignis* is a close relative to the human parasite *D. medinensis*, more commonly known as the Guinea worm. Infestation by the Guinea worm is caused by drinking infected water, and results in painful ulcers on the feet as the worm emerges from the victim. In 1986 this disease affected 3.5 million people. In 2016, there were just 25 cases worldwide. (Greenaway, 2004)

ANOTHER FINE MESS

I do have one last story. Everybody wants to know: what was it like to go to school at the University of Georgia during the 1970s?

Reckitt-Benckiser Group, PLC

Reid Hanson and Dr. Ostrowski, I want you to say this is true. At UGA, there was a renal physiologist by the name of Delmar Finko. No kidding, that was his last name: Finko. It fit his personality. I don't have a picture of him, but he looked just like the picture of Satan on a can of Red Devil Lye[32] [*laughter*].

---

[32] Lewis Red Devil Lye was a drain cleaner taken off the market in 2007, purportedly due to its illicit use as an ingredient in the manufacturing of methamphetamine. (Northrup, 2008)

He had a goiter.[33] It was the first person in the world I had ever seen with a goiter. They had him assigned to teaching clinics, so I had a whole month with Delmar Finko. The one thing I remember learning from him was, "Don't just stand there, son, do something!"

We would have rounds after lunch, and he would eat his grapes one at a time. I hadn't been to lunch and I wanted one of those grapes so badly. Reid—am I wrong? He was so bad—wasn't he, Dr. Ostrowski?—that they eventually took him off of clinics! He was not allowed to be around students.

During rounds, we had pay phones back then. You'd put a dime in the pay phone and you got to

---

[33] Goiter is the medical term for a swollen neck caused by an enlarged thyroid gland. The condition is usually caused by an iodine deficiency. (British Thyroid Foundation, 2008)

call somebody. Well if you screwed up in rounds, Finko would give you a dime and tell you to go call your mother and tell her that you would *never* be a veterinarian. Now you think y'all have stress. That is the truth. That's the truth!

[*After another drink of tea*] When I was on clinics, we had an intern doctor and we had Dr. Finko, so we had two cases per time slot. Now, the object of the game was to get a thorough history and a thorough physical exam and get out in that hall and get the intern, Dr. Middleton, before the other student got Dr. Middleton first. The losing student got stuck with Dr. Finko. That's how it worked.

I did get one case with him one time, and I've got to tell you about it. I love this. I had a dehydrated

Dachshund, and I was SOAPing my case[34], and I said, in front of Dr. Finko, "Today, the dehydration is much better." [*Shaking his head after a beat*] That was wrong [*laughter*].

Dr. Finko of course wanted me to say something along the lines of, "The dog's *hydration* status was much better." But at the time, Dr. Finko looked at me and he said "Now, Charlie. You went to Clemson. Would you really say, 'The dehydration is much better?' "

And I said to myself, Dear God in heaven what does this man want? So I thought and I thought and I thought, and then I said, "The dehydration

---

[34] SOAP is a problem-based way of keeping medical records, and stands for Subjective, Objective, Assessment and Plan. Each of the patient's problems receive a separate SOAP in the medical record, in which the doctor describes the problem—both subjectively and objectively—assesses the severity and possible cause of the problem, and describes a treatment plan. The SOAP method is used in almost all human and veterinary hospitals today. (Lee Jacobs, 2009)

are much better!" [*roaring laughter*]. No kidding. That's God's honest truth.

Anyway, some years later I went to see him and I told the secretary, "Tell him that the worst student he ever taught in vet school is standing out here in the hall."

She went in and told him, and I heard his voice say, "There's too many of them!"

Anyway. Another fine mess.

Ladies and gentlemen we are coming to the end. Emily, hit the next slide.

The Big Toss

My daughter was a majorette in high school. When they finished the halftime show, there was always the big toss. And this is a thinking exercise, now. Dr. Johnson, do you know who that fella on the screen is? Dr. Johnson knows.

But let me tell you, this gentleman was a professor of history, dean of the graduate school, and in 1892, he brought football to Alabama Polytechnic Institute.

Who is that? Who? Come on. Who is it?

George Petrie.[35]

He did a lot of great things. What is the one thing that I have not talked about tonight? The Auburn Creed, that's right. He wrote the Auburn Creed.

---

[35] Dr. George Petrie, who taught at Auburn from 1887 to 1942, is most famous for having written the Auburn Creed (which can be found at the end of this book) in 1943, and for bringing football to Auburn in 1892. The first Alabamian to ever earn a PhD, Petrie also founded both the History Department and the Graduate School, taught history and Latin, and served as the Dean of the Graduate School. (Jernigan, 2007)

Courtesy of Wikipedia Commons

Just like when I went on *Antique Roadshow*, I've done my homework. I'm not gonna talk about the

Auburn Creed, because I've got something a little bit better [*pulls out a piece of paper and reads*].

> *In June, 1947, just a few months before his death, George Petrie gave an interview to a young correspondent from the* Auburn Alum News. *Listen to what Petrie said: "I once heard a man say that it is a very great thing to commit one's destiny to the keeping of a great institution," the 81-year-old man told the young student journalist. "I can testify to the truthfulness of that remark."*

[*Speaking again*] Ladies and gentlemen, I've been doing this for 34 years and 7 months. It has been an honor to commit my destiny to the keeping of this great institution. That's the big toss, right there. It's not the Auburn Creed.

Remember, you're keeping it too, this great institution. Alright, Emily hit the last one.

[*A still of another video clip appears on the screen.*]

This is Conrak leaving the island. He got *fired* for taking these children across the water to Beaufort, South Carolina so that they could enjoy Halloween. They didn't know what Halloween was, okay? At the end of this, they're going to be playing Beethoven—*Dun dun dun DUNNNN*—kids called him Clay-thoven. It meant death and I don't like that particular analogy, but anyway, let me show you what it is.

[*The video plays*]

> *"It hurts very badly to leave you. My prayer for you is that the river is good to you in the crossing."*

[*Boat engine starting, Beethoven's 9th beginning to play*]

I don't like that ending, so I've chosen a more appropriate song for our ending, by the Beatles. Hit it, Emily.

[*"There Are Places I Remember" by the Beatles plays over the speakers. At the conclusion of the song, the room is silent. Dr. Hendrix speaks once again.*]

I love you almost as much as I love my own daughter. Thank you for coming.

[*Audience applauds extendedly, a standing ovation*]

Auburn Photographic Services

The Auburn Creed

"I believe that this is a practical world and that I can count only on what I earn. Therefore, I believe in work, hard work.

I believe in education, which gives me the knowledge to work wisely and trains my mind and my hands to work skillfully.

I believe in honesty and truthfulness, without which I cannot win the respect and confidence of my fellow men.

I believe in a sound mind, in a sound body and a spirit that is not afraid, and in clean sports that develop these qualities.

I believe in obedience to law because it protects the rights of all.

I believe in the human touch, which cultivates sympathy with my fellow men and mutual helpfulness and brings happiness for all.

I believe in my Country, because it is a land of freedom and because it is my own home, and that I can best serve that country by "doing justly, loving mercy, and walking humbly with my God."

And because Auburn men and women believe in these things, I believe in Auburn and love it."

—Dr. George Petrie, 1943

Acknowledgements

Many thanks to Dr. Hendrix, for being kind and generous with his time in helping me prepare this book. Thanks to the Auburn Student Government Association and the individuals who organized this lecture in the first place: Emily Warman and Katie Xu Sedlaczek from the Class of 2017, as well as Bradley Lawson from the Class of 2018. Thanks also to Dean Calvin Johnson for helping me to locate historical information on the towering figures of Auburn's veterinary school, to everyone who proofread my drafts, and to my high school newspaper adviser Mrs. Denita Hines for teaching me almost everything I know about journalism and design. Last, thank you to all my friends who encouraged me to spend what little free time vet students have on getting this done and who promised they'd buy a copy if I did (if you're reading this, I hope that means you followed through).

About the Font

Georgia is a friendly and humble typeface designed in 1993 by Matthew Carter as a serif counterpart to the sans serif font Verdana. Georgia takes its name from a tabloid headline that read, "ALIEN HEADS FOUND IN GEORGIA," in reference to a skull-shaped object that was inadvertently excavated by workers in Alma, Georgia. The font shares many characteristics with Times New Roman, but Georgia is generally wider, with blunted, flat ends. Other slight alterations improve Georgia's readability at small point sizes. (Grodske)

About the Author

Matthew Everett Miller was born and raised in Bowling Green, Kentucky. After graduating from Bowling Green High School, he attended Vanderbilt University, where he studied Biological Sciences and Philosophy. He began classes at Auburn's College of Veterinary Medicine in the fall of 2015. The following summer, he was selected as an AAAS Mass Media Fellow, which allowed him to work as a science journalist for *Slate* magazine for 10 weeks. He is due to graduate from Auburn in May of 2019.

Comments, questions or corrections can be sent to him via email at matthew.miller@auburn.edu

Follow him on Twitter: @miller_writes

References

Addady, M. (2016, August 26). This Is How Much Americans Spend on Their Dogs. *Fortune*.

Anderson, L. C. (2015). *Laboratory Animal Medicine*. Elsevier.

Auburn Athletics. (2014, September 2). *MCGOWEN TO MCGEHEE: A JORDAN-HARE STADIUM FIRST*. Retrieved from Auburn Tigers Football: http://www.auburntigers.com/sports/m-footbl/spec-rel/090214aae.html

Auburn University. (2007, January 7). *Former Auburn Swimmers Denniston and Gaines Receive NCAA Awards*. Retrieved from Auburn Tigers: http://www.auburntigers.com/sports/c-swim/spec-rel/010707aaa.html

Auburn University. (n.d.). *Faculty Directory*. Retrieved from Auburn University College of Veterinary Medicine: http://www.vetmed.auburn.edu/faculty/hendrix-charles/

Biography. (2015). *Fred Astaire: Mini Biography*. Retrieved from Biography.com: https://www.biography.com/people/fred-astaire-9190991

Boyd, C. T. (2011). The lost history of American veterinary medicine: the need for preservation. *Journal of the Medical Library Association*, 8-14.

British Thyroid Foundation. (2008). *Thyroid Nodules and Swelling*. Retrieved from British Thyroid Foundation: http://www.btf-thyroid.org/information/leaflets/32-thyroid-nodules-and-swellings-guide

Davis, J. H. (2016, November 5). The Closer: Michelle Obama. *The New York Times*.

Greenaway, C. (2004, February 17). Dracunculiasis (Guinea Worm Disease). *Canadian Medical Association Journal*.

Grodske, K. (n.d.). *Alien Heads Found in Georgia*.

Guarino, B. (2016, October 4). Screwworm outbreak in Florida deer marks first U.S. invasion of the parasite in 30 years. *The Washington Post*.

Harding, S. (2015, November 15). Mary Nolin Greene. *Auburn Pub*.

Hendrix, C. M. (n.d.). *Obligatory Myiasis-producing Flies*. Retrieved from Merck Veterinary Manual: http://www.merckvetmanual.com/integumentary-system/flies/obligatory-myiasis-producing-flies#v3279247

Hohenstatt, B. (2014, March 18). East Alabama dancing fundraiser has Auburn Veterinary Medicine connection. *Wire Eagle*.

JAVMA. (2017, January 15). Letters to the Editors. *Journal of the American Veterinary Medical Association, 250*(2), 147-150. doi:10.2460

Jeffcoat-Trant. (2015, March 21). *Welcome to the Memorial Page for Dr. Robert L. Carson, Jr*. Retrieved from Jeffcoat-Trant Funeral Home: https://www.jeffcoattrant.com/notices/DrRobert-CarsonJr

Jernigan, M. (2007). *Auburn Man: The Life and Times of George Petrie*. The Donnell Group.

Larson, E. (2014, February 7). *Dr. Leroy Coggins Dies at 81*. Retrieved from The Horse: http://www.thehorse.com/articles/33362/dr-leroy-coggins-dies-at-81

Lee Jacobs, M. (2009). Interview with Lawrence Weed, MD-- The Father of the Problem-Oriented Medical Record Looks Ahead. *The Permanente Journal*.

Lowe, F. (1995, March 4). He Inspired a Veterinary Renaissance. *New York Times*.

McCabe, J. (1965). *Mr. Laurel and Mr. Hardy*. Plume.

McCarter, M. (2011, January 6). Auburn's 1957 national championship came from nowhere. *AL.com*.

Northrup, M. B. (2008). *What is Red Devil Lye*. Retrieved from eHow: http://www.ehow.com/about_5387620_red-devil-lye.html

Roberts, D. (2006). *British Hit Singles and Albums (19th ed.)*. London: Guinness World Records Limited.

Rutgers University Center of Alcohol Studies. (n.d.). *Howard W. Haggard (1891-1959)*. Retrieved from Rutgers University: http://library.alcoholstudies.rutgers.edu/archives/howard-w-haggard

Solomon, A. (2016, March 11). The Middle of Things: Advice for Young Writers. *The New Yorker*.

Sports Reference. (n.d.). *Rowdy Gaines*. Retrieved from Sports Reference: https://www.sports-reference.com/olympics/athletes/ga/rowdy-gaines-1.html

Taylor, M. (2015). *Veterinary Parasitology, Fourth Edition*. John Wiley & Sons.

The New York Times. (2008). *Hardcover Advice*. New York.

University of Pennsylvania. (1984). *School of Veterinary Medicine: A Brief History*. Retrieved from University Archives & Records Center: http://www.archives.upenn.edu/histy/features/schools/vet.html

Vietnam Veterans Memorial Fund. (1969, 11 May). *James Etheridge Greene Jr*. Retrieved from The Wall of Faces: http://www.vvmf.org/Wall-of-Faces/19864/JAMES-E-GREENE-JR

Weaver, A. (2008, February 10). Auburn University building names, namesakes. *OA News*.

Made in the USA
Columbia, SC
29 April 2025